F/O Phibble

No Loneliness

Temple Cone

is this speaker you?

Awarded the 2009 FutureCycle Poetry Book Prize

Question:
① how often do you
write new poetry?

what do you teach
② @ Navy?

FutureCycle Press
futurecycle.org

No Loneliness

Published by FutureCycle Press
Mineral Bluff, Georgia, U.S.A.

ISBN: 978-1-938853-15-9

For Shannon & Isabelle

root & blossom

Contents

There is no loneliness like theirs.

—James Wright

Considerations of Earth and Sky

Begin talking through the pain, not with it.
Point out the nail in the stranded post,

rusting, fenceless, like despair. Or the cows
who obey thunder's psalm by kneeling down.

Give it a name. Any name. Try creek-flood,
brush fire, snowstorm. You compound suffering

with the plain beauty of a world we're not meant for,
and you get suffering. Compounded.

Try words washed clean as pebbles. Think *fjord*.
There's a keen redtail up in yonder spruce.

When old men drive by, don't try to match their stares
that measure you like a dipstick does oil;

just notice how the Chevy's prime and rust,
shining through the white paint, correspond

to an Appaloosa's spots. Horse of stars.
Bless anything well-made, the north wind says;

don't romance without a good four blankets.
Hunger's a challenge at first, then a joy,

then a tool you remember to carry
everywhere. Almost ordinary, till one day

you're walking an empty highway, past rockwalls
maybe ten million years old. You look up—

granite stained with bird-lime, lichen, freeze cracks—
and realize you could eat the goddamn clouds.

River

Eventually, all things merge into one, and a river runs through it.
—Norman Maclean

All I know of heaven is a river,
brackish, running slow under bleary sun.
Humid days. Still, mute nights. No angels there,
just cormorants perched along a bridge-span
or gnats choiring above the water's glare.
Even in dreams, I'm haunted by the flow
of tides. Their currents, steady as love, bear
both the sunburst clouds and their shadow.

Along the river and the river's edge,
barn swallows arc and cross, sweeping the sedge
for twigs or string to fret into a nest.
Now two pass, knitting the distant blue sky.
Like hands at prayer, they grasp the mystery
of this life, lonesome, shared, with which they're blessed.

For Nell & Jim McCarty

Rappahannock

Summers along the Rappahannock,
first light slivered electric towers
on whose trusses perched
cormorants, drying
their green-black wings.
You could lean back in a rocker,
smell brackwater heating up
as crickets scraped
under the porch, the dawn
washing over beach flats,
sea-oats, plantain, parched reeds,
then whitening to a glare so hard
the oyster scows seemed ice-locked,
as if watermen could step over
their gunwales and walk.

You'd begin to see
dark lines of wharves stretching from shore,
the wrecks of trawlers
speckled with gulls and gull-shit,
diesel fumes risen from the wake
of johnboats over slick brown water.
Grackles sing in the sweet gums,
sing like torn metal,
your face glazed with a second skin
of sweat as you wade out,
swim through drifts of nettles
toward the stanchion
you moored the boat against overnight.
You grip the side, pull yourself
dripping onto the bleached deck,
steer through waterways
of widgeon grass and deep channels,
learning the shape of the river.

Wharf

Was my father's word. The rain-warped wood,
a shoddy ladder stretching from dank sand,
lured me as a child. Some nights I stood
watching the far shore, my back to the land.

I'd see oyster scows on the river, home
after a long day scouring empty beds.
Looking for cast-offs, gulls trailed like foam,
starboard lights flickering a burnt-out red.

The planks were speckled with nettles, ghost-trails
gaffed and laid aswirl to dry in sun.
A broken road. Ossuary of scales.
Bridge the builder couldn't fit to span

water the wind wrinkled like a crumpled page.
When winter storms tore gaps as big as boys,
I'd help my father, or rather watch him, patch
old wood with new. He'd fit blond boards to joists

stippled with rust blooms where the nails had been.
Hammer curled back like a bright steel claw,
he squared up wood-screws and drove them clean.
Better hold, he said. Once, I'd had to bow

over the edge with him, to scrape barnacles
from a piling. I asked if he worried
the pier wouldn't last. One flick sent shells
into the waves, and he straightened, a board

himself. Hand to the sun, his face grew dark,
fixing me for a moment in his glance.
It's a wharf, he said, then bent to his work
again. And I have not forgotten since.

The Apple-Knocker

—after a painting by Carroll Cloar

There's a boy in overalls
sitting up in the apple branches.
I don't play much
around him, but he watches me,
calicoed in shadow
by the whitish apple leaves
blowing about
him like loose cotton.
And when mother calls me
to bed, I never ask,
but he's out there after dark,
waiting where porch-light
leaves the trees, a spider
on a mobile of stars.

Romantic Fever

A little wind, the door open, and light
shining across the bed to the corner,
to the old rocking crib, faint roses
sketched from pattern books lining its rails.
The painted eyes of my sister's dolls
stared through bars cast by cradle-light.

I felt my mother sit beside me,
her shirtsleeves' mustardy smell of Old Bay
and crab enveloping me like steam. Downstairs,
a bushel-load of bluecrab rattled the pots.
Voices. My family calling her back.
Claws scraped the metal walls.
                              *I've got Romantic
fever, don't I?* All day I'd slept, white-hot
sheets clinging to me like dreams of drowning,
where the body never touches bottom.
Below the collarbone's arc, a trilling,
my heart panting to fly
                              its white cage.
Romantic, I whispered, as she pressed a cloth
to my face, water tinged with lime and bourbon
that stung before it rose from the skin.
Under the sheet, her fingers ran along
the narrow channels of my side, sounding,
as if her hands could find the true depth.

In the river floated broken shells,
drifts of them, dumped, red peels like tiny cuts
turning white under the moon, white as snow
falling on the moon. I watched the current
swirl them, water filling empty joints
the dark swallowed, piece by piece, like moths
night takes back after the porch lights cease.

Summer Job

I can't touch wood without remembering
that summer in my uncle's lumber mill.
We rolled back punch-in time just to win
an hour of dark, to cross the concrete yard
with only the slightest halo of sweat.
Inside the warehouse, though, we met heat
that hadn't unstifled overnight,
that made even dry pine resin again.
Back then, all I wanted was to get away
from the men I worked beside, who joked too hard
with me, straight from college, and didn't read
Keats over lunch. The youngest, they made me
climb three stories to where the choice wood lay
in bins twenty feet deep. Hand over hand,
I scaled ladder-rungs rubbed smooth by decades
of men hauling themselves up a tight shaft
between catwalks. Up there, under the eaves,
the air flecked with dust, some of it wood, some
of it probably skin, shed years before,
and me breathing it in. From down below
came cries for *white oak rail* or *crown molding*,
the words muffled, but sure, like hymns in church.
I'd scan unlabelled bins, guessing by grain
or design, then yell back for the boardage.
Three-hundred feet, it'll be a huge staircase.
All around me, on the heavy rafters,
men had written out simple calculations
to judge how many boards each house would need.
Even beams I pulled from the stacks were inked
along the edge with a calligraphy
of division: tallies, sometimes scratched out,
but never, never wrong. What was asked for
was always delivered. To callused palms,
the smooth wood felt almost cool. When it slid
over the rail, into the empty space
above the warehouse floor, I'd listen
to that faint hiss the new wood made, crossing
the old, would feel it tilt, the axis reached,
down to the dark, to the sure hands below.

Service

My last summer at the mill, I'd drive
to the Byrd Park courts after dark, serve
buckets of balls to work the tightness
from my arms. The racquet's rubber grip
cooled split skin, bristle-furred balls
loosening my left hand's tired fist.
I'd start at deuce, each swing
lost among the pick-pock play
of other courts. Under the canopy of lights
moths roiled like applause. It helped to believe
someone waited on the other side,
a face in the snowfall of hazy light:
Becker, Borg, Ashe, my father sometimes,
who'd gotten me this job, who'd taught me
to swing through every shot
even if playing alone. Each serve was a splinter
pried from my hand, a stack of pine-boards
I could set down. Balls ran like stones
from a sling-shot, bit the ground and kicked clean
into night. The hours I was there
I learned the ache doesn't dull
but goes on burning,
that there are motions like wingbeats
in which we can rest, washing sweat with sweat.
The humid air breathed *toss, kneel, release.*
Whole days poured into that swing.
Then it was gone—the job, the night—
and only the stroke stayed with me
long after the work that blessed it
had been carried away.

The Prodigal

From the delta of wrinkles flooding his cheeks
to the eyes slow as a fly-goaded bull's,
we know what the father wants: his son back.
But what does the boy want? Might as well ask

him for forgiveness. Yet the way he sits,
tongue worrying apple skin from his teeth,
says *No chance.* Later he'll stamp out the back
door, slam it hard, dust covering his tracks.

Those who watch him wonder was it cruelty
or love that let us let the boy have his way.
Why let bones break? Aren't we good? Isn't God?
But with no break, nothing mends. Besides,

it's not about why we fail, the mostly good,
but why we never ask after the boy,
which may account for the stolen whiskey,
his black eye, and why we're only mostly good.

Calf-Bearer

I dreamed myself a calf-bearer last night,
one of those giant, rope-veined statues
excavated from the Acropolis,
a brown calf cloak-like across my back.
It was the long day of sacrifices,
the air filled with fearful bleating, the slick stench
of burned guts, and black flies storming above
the grease flames for a taste. This calf, though,
was calm, its fur still sour with morning milk,
the pale, swishing tongue not raspy but soft
as wet cloth on my cheek. Marble steps climbed
to the altar in hundreds, infinite
but nearing end. I gripped above the hoofs,
waiting for tendons to tense, flinch, buck, kick,
but no struggle came. Amid the ringing knives,
I felt only soft ribs sucking in air,
a dank hay scent blowing against my cheek.
I had fifty more calves to bear up that day.
I remember smiling. I must have been
smiling, distant, archaic, like the marble
statues themselves, whose faces are always
the same, shining, from the terrible knowledge
that sometimes seems like joy, that it is never
their own holocaust to which they go.

Witness

I have seen an arrow pass through the heart
of a deer, and the deer, with a flinch,
continue nosing the moss
that blackened the roots of an oak.
But the deer knelt down, at last,
in damp leaves, cocked his head to hear,
then sagged, paling the earth
with his white throat, his loosening skin.

And I have seen a carpenter,
with his palm pierced in a jig-saw, put down
the half-carved block—the wood
sallow as flesh stripped bare—
and so as not to snap the blade, pull it
clean through the webbing of his hand,
his eyes raised the way the murdered look
to the sky, as vague as St. Sebastian's stare.

The dark pines in winter I have seen,
with branches full of snow, conceal
the kerosene drunks
gone to sleep in the shells
of abandoned cars, and I have seen
those men stumble in the woods at night:
their hearts answer one another
like ripples after a stone

with blood that wells from everlasting wounds.

One Crow, a Killing

The men who kill crows know their acts bear
no repeal. Waiting till dusk, they grip
twelve-gauges loaded with shot
and watch the sky for murders
circling the cornfields. A single crow
can ride a stalk to ground,
pry open the husk, the veined silk,
scraped kernels peppering its face
with flecks of white and gold.

The farmers I know won't let them near
the corn, but shoot before they perch.
Some, though, will walk in behind
to see those damned eyes, the iris red
beneath a sheen of black,
and kill them when they try to rise.
With wings stretched out like funeral crepe
they nail them to a fence.

I've seen it done. I've brought crows out
from the corn-rows, the weight of each in hand
swinging with my stride as I walk.
Nothing but a warning, farmers say, *to keep
them out the corn.* No matter how the eye
squints, the bodies of crows mark fences
like blood scrawled on a door.
In a week they dry, black down puffing out
and caught in the wind like milkweed,
blackness iridescent as scales,
the skin too weak to hold.
                            I've seen
what else is done to them in death.
Feet cut off, poked through
and threaded with string for wind-chimes,
the talons clicking hollowly
as crystal. And at Sunday service
when choir and preacher begin to sing,
motes of dust falling like gold in heat,
the women fan themselves with coal-dark wings.

Killings

We'd lost the match, and started home so soon
the kids didn't change or shower. I drove,
the van silent, faintly acid with sweat,
because, as you said, *I'm so fucking mad,*
I'll kill them all. Us too. Nine to sixty-six,
against the best wrestling squad we'd meet
all season, didn't necessitate murder,
but I saw your point, and drove.

                    A storm had moved
in that night, whipping up snow in sheets
that spiraled, clung to fenders and wind-shields,
and spun cars off the road, down banked shoulders.
I counted twelve in an hour.

I'm still not sure where the deer came from.
He might have formed, *sui generis,*
from falling snow. Regardless, I hit him.
The right headlight shattered against his ribs,
the van skidded, and there was a soft bump
as legs and pelvis broke beneath the wheels.
We waited for a minute, then climbed out
and ran down the road to where he lay.
The lights from traffic drew near and passed,
a half-light, in periodic brilliance,
wrapping us, enfolding.

                  There was little blood
in the snow: thin lines from where the headlight cut.
We found the path he'd dug, crawling for cover,
trying to crawl even now, the spindles
of his long legs reaching forward in the snow:
catch, pull, an endless imitation
of motions he'd never use again: a buck
white-tail, young and big, a nine-pointer.

Wait with it, you said, then walked back to the van.
I'd never been this close, never had the chance
to grab a deer's fur and feel muscle
tense beneath, as he tried to fight my hold
and stilled, as if he knew this was how

the end must come: a slowing down, the hurt
of touching ground again and finding it
unfamiliar as dream.
                          I didn't believe
you when you came back, said, *We've got to kill
him, now,* but the lug-wrench in your hand
was sure enough. *Take his waist, right there,
don't let the hooves catch you.* I thought how smooth
his belly was, and tight, how he didn't fight
much in my grasp, but paused, as if listening
for more instruction. I couldn't see
if you touched him, but pulling him tight to me,
I tested his broken side to see what he
could take, and smelled his fur, moist with musk
and snow, as you snapped the wrench again
and again on his neck. He broke free once,
but I followed, pinned him down, and then
it was over. We dragged him, each an antler
in hand, down to the wood's edge, where silence
was, no color, not even lights from the road
to show us where we left him.

For Chris Potter

Starlings

Late rain over the mountains. I run the long road
past the whitewashed church near my house, the grounds
an acre of man-high corn, a crop uncropped
all summer, gold paling to straw. A shriek of starlings

curls above the field, the way water closes after
a stone. Hundreds. A thousand. From the ground,
the starlings resemble the swallows that flew south months ago.
But the starlings are not swallows. They swarm empty trees

at night, leaves culled out of darkness, and their song
fills the roads like the ring of guns in winter,
an angry report of metal in the cold which drops off, quiet.
Even crows fear them. A swallow's wings are velvet, not silk,

and catch the rough fingers that smooth them.
I shot a swallow once, when I was a boy, then cupped its body
in my hands. Now, while starlings wheel overhead,
twilight soft sifts to the ground, curling around me

the way the shadowy starlings canopy the trees.
The crown of the swallow is blue. Not the blue
of rain-capped mountains, nor of gunmetal in full light.
The swallow's crown is sapphire, deep as empty sky.

Quickening now, I pass an oak summer squalls tore down.
Its leaves have turned color with the other trees,
as if they didn't care about the storm, and covered the oak
in a quilt of red and brown, the color of dried blood,

of rust, of the down of the swallow's throat. *O child,*
what did you think the shadows would say?
The rains will still fall. The starlings will still come
at night, and sing beneath your window.

Child, there are words written on the heart
of things that never come to mastery, words indelible
as the call of birds in winter. And it is the heart
that stutters these words. The heart stutters to speak them.

The Handgun Rules

Face facts: you touch it, you're ready to kill.
Talk all you want about the sensuous
gleam of barrel, diamond-notched pommel,
or icy balance gathering in your wrists,

there's nothing staving off nothingness
save an eyelash trigger. The gun's a guard
against, as well as a fulcrum of, force.
You'd best keep it, like your own head, bowed.

Oh, there may come a night, door picked open,
your sleeping wife and child under threat,
when some rough angel says you must end
another man's life, but know this: the debt

of lovingkindness you run up must be paid
with zeroes in the bone that never fade.

Song

My father points to a wooden road
I've never seen,
each plank a casket,
each casket closed, all
those shut lids.

There is a tiger, glaring
with blood.
Here is the road, bearing you
off to him.

I don't want to go,
how can I not, every step
opening a casket,
a little boy inside, buried in soot,
the tiger licking each clean.
O his black tongue, my white neck.

Quandary Farm

The morning came and went.
Long shadows were lifted, set
angel-like on pine-tops,
white-crowned clover swaying in the yard.
By the door, tinging wind-chimes
I bought once for a gift
never sent.

Missing the day, I go down
to the stables. A haze
of hay-dust pools at my feet.
The horses are in Charleston,
their training done, steeplechase season
closing in. Dark stalls, stacked bales,
a bridle hangs from a wall.

And in the pastures, the chicory's blue
pointillist flowers open again.
Each lasts a day. Come evening,
they'll curl tight as spiders
wintering under eaves.

Autumn, and all
the breads I can bake,
are weeks away. The poplars, too,
have sensed it, their yellow leaves
marked purple along the stem.
Tonight I'll lie on blue sheets,
restless as the robins
who sing before dawn.

Mercy

Leaner than the gray French lops
I'd raised as a boy, the wild hare
I held in the August heat
was speckled yellow and brown
as old sandpaper, his pelt
worn to cussedness.
He lay twitching on asphalt
a minute after I swerved
and still hit him.
               I watched
his crazy dance to see
if he would rise, then gathered him,
trembling, into my arms,
one hand on his feather-quill ribs,
the other cupping soft neck.
Dumb luck, this. His eyes lolled
skyward, showed me
what to do. I whispered
some nonsense under my breath,
words to calm one of us.
The sparrow heart drummed in my palm.
I hadn't forgotten how
to end life, could feel the old fracture
of knowledge in my bones.
So when he sprang free,
bounding to a roadside hedge,
I knelt down in the dust,
gaping at my torn shirt, marked skin,
stunned by how quickly
mercy could break from my hands.

Forgiveness

I've heard that deaf children,
in a room where music is played,
grow calm, begin to rock slightly
as the sounds, moving through air,
move them, too. It's this way
with forgiveness; it goes unheard
for a while, delivers us
into a rhythm we can't help,
like a weather front. In the end,
we can't even say
who gave or received, only that air
still trembles, that walls fold around.

① did all your
poems based on
things happening
in your life

② when poems
are inspired by
other

Still Life with .38

Where normally you'd expect honeydew
flecked with a resin of ants,
here the grip's grooved diamonds
show smoothness from years of fitting close
to a single palm. Faint scratches line the barrel,
straight as chrysanthemums
that last a few days before their petals
drop like beads of water from a steamed glass.

A handful of brass-mitered bullets lies scattered
where the silver blades of brook trout
should be. One casing, spent, points upright.
The cleaning kit's open,
a long-handled wire brush, stain-darkened cloth
and small blue vials of oil and solvent
spread out in a crescent,
the ritual complete.

But even at the barrel's tip, there's a smudge
of gunpowder black as a fly.
In time, it will eat through finish
and mar the caliber,
but for now it's only a mark of ash
from an afternoon of plinking cans off rails
thirty yards away, the gun suddenly live
as lightning or a snake in the hand.

Moonrise

How many sacrifices has this milky light
made beautiful for watchers-on?
Lilac sweetens the air, and its leaves,
little hearts or arrowheads or Lucifer tails,
nod gently as I pass. At ease with my century,
I watch cargo-planes across a cornfield
creep like rooting pigs, until they leave the ground
with a shriek.
             At home, I listen
to chants written a thousand years ago,
voices etched onto fragile disks of light, light
we cherish above all else, Vermeer our iconographer,
his interiors suffused with whatever
we long for—peacefulness or grace or hope—
never noticing the darkness the room must be in
for the woman weighing pearls in a scale,
Judgment herself, to be touched with gold.

Wintering

There's an owl that barns here
out of season. It's a way with him,
as with the gleaners in old oils
who hoist bushels and bend
to the grain. Silver-shawled,
he winters alone in the hayloft.

Sometimes when you've lashed bales
on a flatbed for forking in quiet fields,
the owl looks everywhere at you,
lamplight to your steaming face.
You wait in the straw, wishing those eyes,
like blank coins, would test and free you:
that sight, which finally does not come.

A Prayer for the Body

Of all I have desired in prayer,
most has been for the dead, or else,
for those far off—for my grandparents, peace;
for my mother, health;
that my father take pleasure
in more than the love of work;
that my wife dream of me.
Praying, I open my hand out over space
and say to lights unreachable as stars,
Grab hold, I will pull you in.

But once, when I dragged the body
of a deer from the road, slipped
and fell against his side,
the fur wet and cold as clay,
I thought how prayer goes out
of the body, forgetting the weak impulse
of tissue, forgetting the tender fat
whose pleasant, unwanted folds
first tell the soul that life is secure
enough to hope for others.

So let me cramp painfully
that I may better love
my mother, my sister, my wife.
Let my muscles slacken, my skin loosen,
so when I brush my father's shoulder
I will know whom I touch.
Beneath these clothes, I am glad
to be naked, without mirror, without looking
on myself in secret pride
or humiliation.   I wait to be opened
like milkweed on a long road,
and spread, a gift of flesh, across the night.

For my family

After Donne's Devotions

What falls? Another January
snow—over the lake,
a skein of mallards

dropping, like the piano's
felt-lined hammers,
in glissando—

each skips once
on the water, chest out,
wings folded behind,

to emerge, swimming,
the change liquid
as a mouth shaping words—

cittern to Bach to
snowdrop. The white woods
begin to fill

with bell-notes,
the church just out
of sight, striking one, two,

and in its toll,
the lesson's passion—
stand, stand—

the rest falls away.
And this is heard,
a waking song

from years past,
saying, in silence, go
in grace.

Lent

In February's dark hour, we choose to leave
behind those things we cling to
most—drink, smokes, meat, a stubborn love
of baseball—to cleanse the heart forty days
before spring breaks open in cherries.
To see the small, soft cup of white flesh
in a flake, or dream of hanging up our scarves—
that is why we send our loves away.

Our time is lent to us, portioned out
in ways we'd weep to understand. The call
of geese at dawn can ease us, or a friend's voice
remembered like the whisper of feet over snow.
But even these we have to give away,
for they were only ours to borrow.

In memory of Andre Dubus (1936–1999)

Churches

The abandoned ones end up like weathered barns,
the sort you see from the road and dream of,
forgotten places you'd never actually fill
with horses or the labor of your own hands,
because who'd want to invest in a ruin?
Yet you walk in one day, watch dust turn gold
in the light of those achingly simple windows,
run your hand along the stalls, the wood
still coarse as if raised only yesterday,
and breathe the air. Someone was here,
kneeling down in a bed of dry hay, working
pieces of iron from the curve of another's feet.

Theory

Before I listen to you,
explain that eagle, trapped on the lake
near an ice-fisherman's hole,
that dark lily tearing frantically
at its frozen shins.

Whether you like it or not,
you have to step in the same river twice.
There is no other world.

When wind blizzards through firs,
a hollow forms
beneath the inner branches, where deer go
to wait out the storm. Don't ask me how
the deer know to do this.

Just follow your own cold bones.

A spring ephemeral
will tunnel through feet of old snow
to bloom under
the shifting March light. To guard
its nest, a blue jay
will adopt the redtail's cry.

For years, I've clasped trout
behind their gill-vents,
slit their long, white waists, and tossed
ropey guts on shore
for the minks and osprey. I'm glad
my hands lived those things.

It took forever, and then took nothing
at all. Remember that. Before learning
to speak, the tongue first lives
as a muscle. Remember that.

Gambrel

Offers the most beautiful shelter
of any word I know.
Think shingles
cut from cedar, the amber resin
of pitch-pine for caulking.

No wonder the Cooper's hawk,
chased from fallen timber,
returns as a barn owl
to ghost its heavy rafters.

The hay and climbing heat
bring forth a fragrance
like the idea of God finding us.

Whoever thought to build
a roof with the look of rain streaming
off a horse's back
could never have dreamed
the tongue would find its equivalence.

Through eighty-degree dawns, through blizzards,
the air inside maintains absolute pitch.
The dead men who raised it
still linger in the dust.

A lifetime won't cave it in.
Yet when the beams do fold, I pray
I'm gone on some prairie,
out where pasqueflowers can push through
the snowdrifts of my spine.

The Story About Horses

My mother asks me for a story about horses.
I stare into her small, dark face
and think, *I don't know a thing about horses,*
which isn't entirely true, I've lived beside a pasture
where a stable of thoroughbreds wintered.
Sometimes at night they'd kick open the gate,
a hammer striking stone.
I'd wake and go out, nicker them back to the field,
guiding them by the bridle like sleepwalkers.
It's not familiarity that's missing, but a sense
of the loyal opposition
I imagine rodeo hands and horse trainers possess.
I've ridden horses, washed them, forked hay
and cleaned stalls, which isn't so bad,
just a closeness
like you breathing from their lungs, and they yours.
But I've never had to lay hands on one
out of necessity, knowing
if I didn't break that colt soon, he'd grow wild
and maybe toss someone I loved.
I'm lucky that way. I get to touch them
gently, stroke the skull's long plain of bone,
which is what I try to tell my mother prevents me
from telling a story about horses.
There needs to be hardship, and pain, and any love
that grows out of this will flourish
like a weed, outlasting
late-May frosts and 96° in the shade.
But I realize from the way she's looking at me
this is the story she's wanted to hear,
not about horses, but me,
what it's like to breathe inside this flesh
that came from her,
only you can't tell a story like that outright,
you have to use another one,
about horses,
about how lucky it feels
to have straddled broad ribs
and moved above the ground for an hour or two,

or how you don't have any good horse stories
because life hasn't crushed you
the way the love that loves horses requires,
so you can only make sense of their peace
when they're alone,
or their patient gaze that drinks up pastures,
white after spring rain.

October

These quiet, dim mornings, I listen
beneath oaks turned red as churned clay
for the emptiness left by birds already miles
distant, chastened by the coming cold.

Practice, the Tao advises, *being still.*
Believe in what you least expect, I say.
Walking beside the paddock, the bitter scent
of crushed walnuts underfoot, I trace a barn swallow

nipping flies off piles of horse turds.
Still here in October. The deep blue coat,
long, bifurcated tail trailing each banked turn,
a twittering for its song, not musical

but busy and glad, an under-the-breath hum
that carries the body through its labors.
I see now the swallow's building a nest,
or finishing up: it flits from piles of straw

to a mud-daub wedged under barn eaves.
Between trips, it perches a bow in the fence rail,
ruffles its wings, and preens. I have to wait
till it slips in the nest hole to get near,

one step each time. When I'm close enough
to see each feather lining its rusty face,
and the damp, black eyes, I'm close enough.
Around us, the leaves go on falling

down invisible threads. If asked, I'd say
each hour's its own season, and just as brief,
but nobody's asking. The swallow's gone now.
I'd say the world, somehow, suffices.

Tea

An old companion, tea
warms our hands, can accept sweetness.
Its steam bends with living breath.

To imagine a war fought over
tins of dry, crushed leaves
is not impossible, however ironic.

Thoreau swore it off, along with coffee, wine.
He believed in the ceremony of cold
spring water and often sat alone.

Practitioners of Zen can focus
an entire afternoon on the whisking
of green tea in little porcelain cups.

Between them, two adepts may speak of nothing
for hours. Yet I prefer the example
of Po Chü-i, who, finding himself

without tea for guests, led them
into his garden. There, he pulled
a peach blossom under

the kettle's steaming lip,
served tea fragrant with the delicate
gold of pollen-dust.

The Recipe

calls for flour, beer, salt, and sugar, a bread tin, and other ingredients, as desired. I twist the cap off a bottle of Yuengling porter, sip it first, a few drops like honey in my beard, then pour the rest in a pot over clumps of flour. The foam bubbles, then seeps through, and the batter thickens. A tablespoon of salt. Two of sugar. Garlic buds, peeled by hand and crushed in a press, the yellowish curds, almost blue, squeezed into the pot. Had you come in the kitchen then, you'd have seen me clean the press of the papery pulps of garlic, rinsing my hands under cold water. But you waited till I'd snapped shut the oven door, then snuck behind, circled your arms around my chest, your mouth against my shoulder, breathing warmly through my sweater. I could almost turn back to smell your hair, but ran my hand instead from your hip to your ribs, pulled loose your shirt and brushed my fingertips against your side. When we opened the oven, the elements burned red as tanagers. You took the first slice from the loaf, still too hot, and mumbled, mouth full, words escaping like steam, *My God, it's wonderful, wonderful bread.*

Cherries

The sun and cherry buds came out today
when the snow finally stilled.
Winter, though we never believe it does this,
sometimes warms the air:
the roots feel a spring wetting down;
soil and bough dampen, somehow darken, within;
the buds press the bark like baby's toes, testing
balance in the sun this late January.
Only the cold returns, and the buds, too,
thicken like knuckles on the limbs.
Your hands want to touch the cherry in the blossom
in the bud in the bark of the cherry,
and I will wait for you to taste the sun
in the cherries in your mouth in the spring.

Grace

This was not your normal talk
of giving up, going on
to become an astronaut, litigant,
or double-agent. Doubtless it leapt
in your mind, mingling with thoughts
of something undefinable as grace—
you would become a ballerina.
You're 23, I said, *a bit ossified,*
and besides, you'd be the tallest girl.
You put your foot down then.
Just because you can't—
and when you lifted your leg,
blue jeans and bare feet
in mock-pirouette, I imagined
a column at Delphi, one under
the east eave of the temple to Apollo,
your body threading
heaven and earth. In the silence,
sunstreaks slanted down clouds.
Then you came before me,
neither sibyl nor dream,
but a woman, nubile,
like the statues those mysterious
sculptors made from marble
diaphanous as ribbon.
If you had asked,
I would have bought you shoes.

A Long Stay

Frost blankets the field. Though I come
this way every day, the gray poplars
stand farther off than usual.
The east opens, oriental pink, and slowly
brown, wet sheaves of plantain show
through the frost like cracks in porcelain.

Beside the fence, a doe bows
her slender neck and head.
Wool-must carries downwind,
mingling with bitter musk from deep
in the woods.
                    A truck rigged with ladders
clatters along the road. Turning
up the mossy bank, she faces me,
her muzzle stained wet.

Back in the house, you've packed
for a long stay with family.
Already cold creaks the floorboards,
admits drafts, rattles windows
in their panes. The cat bats pine cones
meant for a wreath. Let missing
these things be a comfort, and not.
I look long at the doe for you.

Out in the field, meadowlarks rise,
quince-yellow in the light,
settle, and rise again. As morning comes,
the ground drinks meltwater,
grasses stand and spread themselves
leaf to pale leaf.

Dreaming in Welsh

The sky is making love to a swan, they say,
and why not, when the town quiets suddenly in a snowfall
as if no one lived there. Shop windows unlit,
the roads clear of traffic, the glow of a street lamp
seems to darken all it touches with its thin light.
Alone in the house, I listen to the soft pittance
of flakes drifting against the storm window.
Outside, a man coasts downhill on a bicycle.
His rear wheel slips slightly as he slows
before my neighbor's mailbox. Through the snow,
I can hardly see if he slides a letter in or takes one out,
or if he simply stares a while into the box.
When he pushes off, the dark rolls in behind him
the way ink blooms in a glass of water, and I reach
for the letter I've just finished writing you. The words
seem fleeting and fallen as the snow, and I worry
how they will sound to you—like the call of whistling swans
or a faint tapping at your window? But I've sealed
the envelope, written the address, even chosen a stamp.
Then I read your name across the front. Your name
is the one, maybe the only, true thing I've written.

Elegy

When the phone rang at noon,
the cows were already gone.
All morning, three men in green jackets
chased them down the far hill,
the sky leaden above. Shrill, white
breaths of bleating calves drifted
and fell.
       The herd was pared.
Some lumbered through a field
of wild carrot and thistle.
The others, chastened, edged
towards an open gate, a trailer ramp.

Later I poured water for tea,
and a little splashed
from the blue-black cup,
scalding the palm of my hand.

In the cold room I stare
at a few blank pages
on my desk. A puff of dust
swirls, lacking the heart
to rise.
       Soon swallows will come
to the barn. Sifting and tilting,
their voices drop with dusk.
In one corner, hay bales
shine like amber beneath the eaves.

In memory of Nelly Watts Ruffin (1909–1997)

Alone at the Equinox

An evening mist seeps through
sun-bleached hayfields, winter's crop.
From the fence, a crow calls rawly,
and peepers ring by the pond.

I used to think music was what happened
when the dark had closed my eyes.
In my Tidewater childhood
every country sound stirred
beneath the night's humid shell:
katydids clicking on a porch screen,
whistle of nightjars in the woods.

Another porch now: I rock a chair,
starlings quieting in trees.
Over the hills, a train whistle sounds
with the long blare of river-tugs
hauling freight on the Rappahannock,
as if that life had followed me here.

                    ❧

If anything, this world is a belief.
Early light, deer shifting
behind a screen of poplars
as they browse for wood-sorrel.

The dog and I climb banks of wet moss,
enter a stillness under the limbs.
I touch the flesh of angel-wing
lining the hollows of a downed trunk,
while she romps, twigs snapping, red muzzle
snuffling the rank dirt.

High in the canopy, winds
creak the thin branches. Two geese
yelp as they dip to the pond,
and there's silver where light touches
a tattered sycamore.

Bluesman

After his first descent to the underworld,
Orpheus didn't die. The Maenads never tore him
apart like an offering of bread,
and the story of his head, singing
as the river bore it downstream to ocean,
is someone's hopeful indulgence
in the persistence of song.
                      What happened
to Orpheus happens to us all.
He wept. He cursed the animals who came
to comfort him, till the woods were silent.
In Thebes, he sold his lyre
and stayed drunk for days.
But the world doesn't stop for myths,
so when the drachmas ran out, he found work
as a gardener. Kneeling hours in the dirt,
he'd talk to trellised morning-glories,
to the crocus and the daisies.
Of course, in time, he began to sing instead,
softly, and without knowing it.
The persistence of song. Then one day
he noticed the flowers following him
wherever he walked, and when he looked,
they didn't turn away.

For Gregory Orr

Heron

A great blue heron flies over the roof
down to the rain-churned pond,
sun on its shell-white neck.

On the Rappahannock as a child,
I watched herons circle the marinas
for cast-off bait and cleanings.
They'd nest on channel markers
in mounds of green limbs and driftwood,
those frail, woven boats.

Stock still in the shallows,
this one spears frogs and red-eye,
shucks snails. At night it settles
under a tall, shagged cedar.

I know the lightness of herons,
all wing and long bone.
I know another will come this spring.
For weeks they'll drift
between here and the pond, inseparable
as swamp lilies wound at the stem.

Love like the Wild Geese

If you do nothing else with your life,
you can do this, you can love like the wild geese.
Because they are simple,
they do not even know what calls them
to the snow-clotted fields in spring,
only that their searing bones
light the way. Because they believe
they are immortal,
they rush over mountains, foothills, meadows
in waves of frightening speed,
since no one wants to live alone forever.
To feel air pulse beneath their wings is a blessing.
To watch two glide on a still pond,
another blessing. Even to see one
flying alone, shorn
of its mate, a kind of blessing,
because they join with their whole lives,
and even in loss cannot be rid of that
outline, always shimmering
at the tip of their outstretched wings.

For Heather Girvin & Chris Potter

Vanishing Point

Horizons have to be learned.
They focus vision
to a chisel's blade-wedge,
so we can chip out
our piece of lonely sky.
When you again
threw off your clothes tonight
with the ease of snow
falling for miles, the roadways blocked,
both of us blanketed in the dark,
I thought of evergreens
stitching a mountain ridge
to the shadowing clouds,
their needles compass points
no one knows to read,
the burnt orange
of your brushed hair
on every one of my shirts.
Your body pressed
next to mine was a dream
of bears waking,
nosing toward blackberries
not yet nippled
with fruit,
the salmon in their blood
endlessly leaping.
Death can't be as final
as your breath closing
over mine
or the distances of your fingers,
miles run at night
on roads lit by nothing
less than risen stars.

Swans

Walking the cindery road
that spring we left the farm,
I felt a shadow pass through me.
When I looked up, I saw

a drift of swans
flocking over the cedar woods.
Then soft bugling fell
all around me.

I don't know why we're afraid
to call this world our own.
All it asks is our attention.
Overhead, the sky swam

like an orchard in a gale.
The swans were lit
by a noon of such pale blue
I've searched everywhere

for the flower
that would give it its name.
I couldn't believe those ships of marble,
their bright, lifting sails,

never knew flight
was not a matter of tilting wings,
but of flinging them
forward into air

in an endless, lasting embrace.

Epithalamion

The bluebell resembles its name,
a small indigo flower
that blossoms downwards
like a dark skirt of rain.

One spring by the river
we found patches of them
on a low bank. In the field guide
you showed me the Linnaean name:
Mertensia virginica.
                    Only later
did I read how they were named
for Karl Mertens, a German botanist,
widowed at thirty-one.

For every flower there are two names,
one common, one learned.
That day by the river
we each knew only one,
but we carried them together
with a kind of faith.

For Shannon Wiegmann

Married

The dirt in Spain baked red. Olive trees
orcharded in long, drowsy rows, silver
dusting the curled blade of each leaf.
Magpies in place of pigeons and crows alike.
Plazas. Wines that savor of words
like *slake* and *brim*. A hundred young men,
dark as bulls, on every street, every night.
The women refusing to walk beside them.
Afternoon cool of cathedrals, or better,
views of the chalk-banked river beyond.
Sweating awake. Then the hour lying naked
together on a sheetless single bed.
Struck bells echoing over the town. The silence
that follows, and the silence after that.

The Miracle Corner

At the unclaimed baggage shop
in Scottsboro, Alabama,

women who aren't ashamed
buy what's lost in the heavens:

shoes stamped with the memory of feet,
dreams of houses stenciled in blue ink,

rings that never get to be married,
red suitcases with nothing inside.

Sometimes a scuffle starts
over a prayer shawl or a child's dress.

A voice awakens to pain.
Then the quiet mends itself back.

In one dust-splotched corner,
wishbone crutches hang from the pegboard,

wheelchairs in stacks,
their leather backs so very straight.

There's a case of false arms,
each laid palm up, palm open

as if to receive a handshake
or a piece of bread.

No one ever comes to claim those,
the clerk admits, *no one ever comes.*

I see them in airports, rising
from seats marked with the sign of the lame

and stepping through glass doors
that part of their own accord.

Specimen Collection

I start with a little cabbage moth
nipped from a crown of white clover,
then gather the dusty, thin-hipped ant
bushwhacking the hair at my wrist.
For a specimen collection, my naturalist wife
asks that I bow to the lower kingdom,
ignoring a while the hawks I love
to trace against the wreckage of clouds,
trading their dark, tiny silhouettes
for a smallness I can grasp in my palms.
Thus, I spend an hour one morning
sifting pond-silt for the ghostly nymphs
of dragonflies, nightmare fleas
whose later incarnations as iridescence
I catch in a willow grove's deep heat
with my long-handled net that's light
as a reed. Stonefly, bumblebee, walking stick,
and a hundred other unnamed things
tumble through its gauze and are emptied
into a jar. Later, she'll arrange the husks,
naming and mounting each in a box.
Her long hands open each dried wing,
never flinching from touch to delicate touch.
One day, walking the neighborhood,
I find a cicada in the grass, a blotchy green
leopard of jade. Lifted, the black wings race,
and a chirring pours from my hands
as if I carried my own heart home.

Loons

Between the islands, our canoe drifted,
a single stroke, now and then, keeping us
poised over the sandy, limb-tangled shallows
that dropped away into fathomless dark.
We couldn't hear waves splash ten feet away—
some trick of sound—but a mother squirrel
chirring in the pines seemed almost as close
as the bright orange vests piled at our feet.

The wind went still. Sun on the nodding lilies
lining the shore softened their yellow heads.
I felt hard words from the night before
spread like ripples, diminishing, then gone,
into the cold water that swirled behind.

When the first loon surfaced, it scanned the lake,
dove back, and rose again with another,
a little farther out, but content, at least,
to let us watch them: velvety black faces,
the throat a band of stripes, the wings a road
speckled under heavy flakes of snow.
These were the ones we heard calling at dusk
when our voices had softened: long, low notes
someone could easily mistake for cries
of grief, if one hadn't heard them before.

Better Stones

Thirst and the odor of scorched weeds have as much
savor as grapes. Last us longer. Not geese, but their absence
in winter. Not the marriage, but the nights of grief.
Like a fracture, definition lies in what is broken.
No wonder Jesus's pain redeems us. At Mass, the bread
is taken without wine. To sharpen the memory of wine.
Better that than the feasts of emperors. Better stones
than fields of gentian. The ocean fills our mouths with salt
to tell us of the streams that feed it. No one dies
having tasted this life. Only having tried.

The Long Day

At the end of the long day,
may shadows find me
leaning against the paddock gate,
watching chickadees bustle seed
from a feeder.
              May heavy rains
bring out sky-blue chicory
while a red-tailed hawk preens
high up in the pines.

At the end of the long day,
may my face be warmed
by low sun off the pond,
my hands chilled by the whisper
of wind inflected with frost.

May the thought of being
scattered among fields,
no longer myself, but everywhere,
calm me in the empty hours
at the end of the long day.

And if the pastoral is an elegy
the soul sings itself—
fields vanishing in pale mist,
moths flushed into the air
by browsing deer—
may it also be without self-pity,
without self,
              a cup
filled with seed or light
at the end of the long day.

In Passing

Each hour's its own season, I wrote once,
wishing, of course, that the best hours could last
long as bayside summers or those Christmas
holidays we remember from years past.

But the proof of happiness is that it's brief.
We mix cakes with salt, listen to sad songs,
squeeze a bit of lemon into our tea,
for no tongue can savor sweetness too long.

Yet some mornings, once May gives way to heat,
we notice hints of gold along the leaves,
or sense, when winter's hold seems complete,
blossoms lodged in icicles under eaves.

So yes, parting's hell, but it's also heaven,
and makes farewell a prayer we can believe in.

What We Call Spirit, What We Call Soul

There are so many places the spirit waits.
Any tree might do. Any road might do.
But the soul is a particular flesh
and thrives on the crumbled moments of a life.
It loves the rented farm's tall sycamores,
angels robed in tattered white and gray,
and the acid scent of walnuts, like sorrow,
crushed under an old workhorse's hooves.

Say the spirit is the whole farm: fields,
the barn that sags in one corner from age,
bats filling the sky, blue morning glories
with hands clasped shut in prayer against the night.
Then what we call the soul is a barn owl
ghosting over high grass, its stained white wings
muting the wind, its eyes drawing light off pines
shadowing the road, off fence posts, off clouds.

Hosanna

Nothing to hosanna, you will be buried
cold. Only the living go on living.

Worship the wind-hover while it's a-wing,
let scything talons fret the meadow grass.

If you bear likeness to the rough face
staring up from a lake, swallow grief, plunge

your hands through, grasp hematite
lining soft silt which like a father's eyes

beckons. Dredge. Repeat. A man thinking on
his dead friend will cast his dry flies

only in shallow pools. A boy, thinking the same,
casts his deep. The wind-soughed woods

and blue-hazed mountains are a bruised prism—
symbols of harm, symbols of healing.

Do not, for a blessing, cross barbed wire
into pastures where ponies graze.

No sugar can sweeten their wildness now.
The question of loneliness comes to this:

whether you go on watching swan-shapes bow
under dry pines to the encroaching dark

or start back down the untrafficked road.

No Loneliness

Some days there's no telling dream vision
from the blear
of too much January light
prisming off *the junipers shagged with ice,* as Stevens would say,
though this is no New England winter,
one part quaint,
              one part Jonathan Edwards's angry God
with the thermostat set way low.
It's Upper Peninsula,
             pure
                  (because no one's around,
not even snowmobiles, whining fiercely
as horseflies)
         and simple
                (because this is virgin wood,
too far north for Chicago to have gone groping
with its butcher's hands
at the black, back end
of the 19th century, and darker days ahead),
                         no Currier, no Ives,
and you'd better not lose the trail,
better not break an ankle,
or it's lights out,
         goodnight, Gracie,
              cue the fat lady.

Not that I'm worried.
I just can't see for all the light,
my rods and cones going all ga-ga
with neon fireflies, tickertape showers of flaked mica,
a zillion neutrinos
cometing through space and matter, the here and now.
In a word or two,
           I'm getting at what St. Theresa was getting at,
how the pain of heavenly love brings

a sweetness so excessive
that one could never wish to lose it.

And I'm desperately happy,
                    like I was happy about God
as a boy, believing
                myself cared for
by a force that ought to have been beyond caring
for such as me,
                as if gravity
or the second law of thermodynamics
had taken a shine to,
                had a soft spot for,
                            gave a shit about me.

I'm snowshoeing
five miles into a yellow birch wood
in the Ottawa National Forest,
                    walking on water, walking on air,
with a little help from the cold,

my wife a few paces behind,
my two friends up ahead, rounding the curved slope
of a kettle hole,
my dumb hound dog bounding by like a snow antelope.

I can even see my daughter, years from being born,
looking back at me,
                just as real
as the blindness I'm seeing,
                the sight that's blinding me.

Sweet Jesus, someone cares.

On My Unborn Daughter's Hands

In ultrasound starlight
the nebulae of my daughter's hands
are shaped by distant winds.

They shield her unseeing eyes.
It isn't water she swims,
it's an ocean of mica.

Radiant, fearful, I stare
at a hospital screen and whisper
through the machine's soft hum,

what do you know of us,
what of your life have you
already seen? Her fingers,

curled starfish, waken and splay.

A Father's Story

That tick at your wrist?
That's time. That body
clutching yours?
That's time too.

The moment light breaks
into snowfall over the water,
the long hour its blood
blossoms in western clouds,
even the river of light and darkness
flowing between, is time.

Grasp this, and every breath
shall make your body sing.
Grasp this, and you shall find
me waiting ahead of you

where our shared road ends.

&

You were not. Then you were.
That cry from your lips
was not pain, as I first believed,
but mortal life everlasting.

Upon every summer leaf is light.
Under every summer leaf is shadow.
The tree knows no difference.
First I was not. Then I was.

&

The moment I first saw
your face, I glimpsed
everlastingness.
Such a strange form of divinity—
instead of one soul
vulnerable to the world's harm,
now there are two.

The amaryllis
with its twinned blossoms
is always the first to suffer
in heavy storms.
Yet the survivors glisten,
brilliant pink
like the first blush of laughter.

The first poem
you ever heard
was Hopkins's
Pied Beauty.

I whispered
those mottled notes
to you in my
hands, minutes old:

He fathers-forth
whose beauty
is past change:
Praise Him.

Beauty, changing
every moment
in my hands,
let me praise

you who fathers me.

Rilke believed love
the reverence
one loneliness holds
for another.

But why cherish
the chrysalis
and not the butterfly
slipping free?

～

Was your soul always with you?
Theologians would argue its presence,
along with all attendant sin.
But I think those first months
you were your soul itself,
the cicada slipped free
of its ghostly skin, awaiting a breeze
to cool the wet, diaphanous wings
into a shape offering flight.

～

God at morning, God at night,
she drinks grace shorn from sorrow,
Celan's black milk stained white
by this child at her mother's breast,
the warmth of another's flesh
on her lips a language
for describing the world.

～

I'm always talking
in long sentences,
trying to fill the emptiness.

Not you. Quiet, or mostly so,
you are the rainy world's well.

Quiet isn't the end of sound
for you, it's the beginning
of the beginning of song.

❧

Your eyes those first months
showed no feeling I have a name for,
though their openness
held the feeling beyond all feeling
I pray God holds for us.

Soon sea-blue faded to sky.
Pleasure, pain, grief, and joy
awakened in your gaze,
spring flowers whose colors startle
even the implacable angels.

❧

To be present to one another.
Nothing harder. Nothing dearer.
The sun, the rain, the darkness
fill the other's face.

This gift surrounds us.
Can't you hear
the raucous choir of finches
calling to each other?

Yet openness is holy
because it can fall away.
What keeps us
from lapsing is love,

love the responsibility
of an *I* for a *Thou*.

❧

Everything is a first for you—
rain, sidewalk, bruise, seagull.
Only the firstness of firsts
is familiar, your native realm.

It is our failing, our falling
that the world of *the*
soon becomes a world of *a*.
So many tears come after.

But one may live here again,
in words where *a* blossoms into *the*,
where even final things
can be felt for the first time.

~

To make a meal
and share it
is communion:

not torn bread
or wine drained
from cups,

but scrambled eggs and toast,
their steam mingling
with our breath.

~

Washing your shiny body
makes me wonder
how this single act
has been repeated
among all people,
as ordinary as prayer.

Not only parents
with children,
but grown children
with frail parents,
lovers the moment before
or the long hour after,
even the sick and wounded.

I see Walt Whitman
through the summer swelter,
bringing moist wraps
to his bloody boys,
cleansing and marking
the last hour of breath.

He must have dreamt
of laying their clothes aside,
wading into a forest pool
to rinse smoke, sweat, salt
of tears from their skin,
then standing together
in that green stillness.

But the washing and dressing
kept those wounds open
in his own side, revealing
the blessing of common acts,
the way a father
is allowed so brief a time

to wash the body of his child.

❧

To keep both our bodies
as they are this instant—
mine still strong,
yours a tiny, unopened bud—

would be to dam the Nile
from flooding its reedy banks
or bring a shade back
through the asphodels of the dead.

Orpheus refused to accept this,
then, resigned, turned suffering
into a song that still echoes
across millennia.

❧

Egg. Your first word.
So you answer the riddle—
the child comes before the parent.
Which fragile shell, I wonder,
do you see when you speak?
The hen's speckled brown oval
or that shard of blue sky,
the broken robin's egg
you plucked from the grass?

I think of John Clare
teaching his own children
the names of songbird eggs,
yellowhammer and pettichap,
liquid hearts beating
under domes streaked
with markings like tiny poems
they have to break through
to be born.

❧

Starling, cardinal, white-throated sparrow, crow,
common grackle, goldfinch, wren, red-winged blackbird,
mourning dove, red-tailed hawk, turkey buzzard,
downy woodpecker, wood thrush, titmouse, chickadee,
great blue heron, blue jay, snowy egret, osprey, barn swallow—
these were all the names of all the birds we saw
one day in your life, when we were together
and the midsummer light was still with us.

❧

Waking this morning
with orioles singing
outside the open window
is a blessing
beyond all blessing,

but holding you
after a long day

of playing in the sun,
your body spent,
your head bowed,

is blessing itself,
never beyond
this moment
or the next,
but here always.

❧

Don't read when you waken,
cautions Rumi. Play
your silver flute instead.

Music wakens the blood,
the sleeping body
within the body.

When I am no longer
there to play
a song for you,

may these words so waken
my memory in you
that you must find a flute

and play me out in song.

❧

When I picture Jesus now,
I think of the pain
he made his parents endure,
his mother clutching his still body,
his father, not God, watching over.

At least Mary felt divinity
welling up from within.
Joseph was left helpless, wanting

to save this child who was his,
but like all children of God, was not.

~

Rilke composed his *Sonnets
to Orpheus* in two months
after finishing the great *Elegies,*
ten years in the making.

So we labor at grief,
drawing constellations from chaos,
and when we pause, gracious
starlight comes unbidden.

~

Do you wonder what it meant
for me to live as myself?
Often I asked the same question
of my father, kind and distant,
who knew engines and figures
as I counted beats and watched birds.
For years, his silence troubled me,
then it did not, and I believed
I had put aside childish things.
But now I see I was waiting
for you to show me
what I ought to become,
just as my father had waited for me.
If you ever wonder what it meant
for me to live as myself,
look to your own heart for answer.

~

Writing these lines without you
in the house, dreaming that time
when I shall no longer be here
with you, my voice echoes

years and years ahead of me,
trying to reach you with all

this hour's loneliness and love.
And through my own words I hear

your voice not yet a voice calling
back to me. Seeking each other,
we find a place where sorrow is not
sorrow, but a shared joy, a song.

&

Does it get any easier?
No. We grow more aware
of every affliction
besetting body and world,
though in time
we grow more aware
of being aware,
a consolation, perhaps
one that will suffice.

&

Of course all this shall be lost.
That's the price of us
rocking together at sunrise,
of a good, cool breeze
on our cheeks at midday.
I will not pretend to be beyond
grief or fear at this,
though I believe such heartbreak
may be part of the savor,
whatever that may say
of joy or sorrow
or of our own hearts.

&

What I love most
about walking with you
is feeling your small hand
when you grasp mine,

not for balance
but simply because I'm close.

　　　　　ॐ

In one of your books
there's a farmer shearing
spring lambs.
They step away
from drifts of fleece,
thin, almost naked,
whiter than before.

The farmer's hands,
bright shears in one,
a lamb struggling in the other,
always make you laugh.
There's no place
in your mind just yet
for suffering.

Or maybe you've already seen
beyond the moment
of pain into the moment
their coats drop
and, freed, they feel
spring's warm light
across their twitchy backs

chasing them into the meadow.

　　　　　ॐ

Holiness is one word
for this radiance,
but there are others—
father, husband, child, beloved.

How good when the words
scatter, as at waking,
when we're simply snow clouds
parting before the sky.

For the longest time I believed
these words could cheat death
and let me stay near you.
But I know it cannot be.
We are all disappearing.

Yet words alone can speak
the word forever, and forever
fades without them.
A rainfall may tell of oceans
the eye cannot see.

So long as you listen, I will be
shaping these words for you.
Even when the book is closed,
the voice goes on
trying to say what it was, is,

and will be when you listen again.

Now That My Daughter Lives in the Sunlight

Now that my daughter lives in the sunlight
the marsh sycamores where our river ends
shine more darkly through their mottled gray.
We have walked this hour under canopied shade,
counting jack-in-the-pulpit and mayapple,
their blooms rust-red and white as bird-lime.
I bear her small body, asleep in my arms,
past man-high cattails freighted with redwings
that flare off like sparks gashed from old embers.
At every step, the petals of her eyes
flicker with the tidal motion of starfish.
The world I know will harm her, as it does
all, and I think how she'll never again be
this safe. When the old heron starts slow
from the reeds and rows to the farther shore,
it seems that trespass haunts us daily.
Kneeling down by the bank, I trail my hand
through a shallow pool warmer than dew,
as if I would christen my daughter
with the salted marsh water, the same salt
as my tears, then think better of it,
and leave her face dry, and her to her dreams.

For Isabelle Cone

The Dream of Meanings

Listen.
I don't know if I'm speaking to you before or beyond the grave.

Words lose their path, like walkers in a dark wood.
Some say words never find the way back, never join the things they
    mean:
cirrus cloud, mercy, foal, seashore, eyelid, grace,
not even love.
           They say each word is elegy to what it signifies,
marker of loss, a gravestone.

I don't doubt our words go astray, miss the crossroads, sit down in
    the rain and cry.
But sometimes I dream, and in that dream, words mean
everything we want them to mean.

Sometimes they reveal the griefs or hopes we kept secret from
    ourselves,
teaching us as they pass over our lips, like a lover's kiss.
Sometimes they are precise as the knife we use to gut the trout,
separating white flesh from dark entrails
to feed our children.

Listen, for our time together is brief, and passing.
In the dream of meanings, I learned what the words meant because I
    believed that the words meant.

I offer no proof. You must have faith, or be silent.

The ones who speak of elegy, of loss and confusion,
say words are a blackberry bramble collapsed upon itself,
unable to bear fruit,
though I doubt they would ever kneel down before a bramble of
    blackberries,
such pliable, thorny wood, such unrefined sweetness,
a shelter for rabbits and mice.

But in my dream, the word is epithalamion to what it signifies,
the wedding-song
our breath takes up as it marries the world,

bride and bridegroom indistinguishable in cool afternoon light,
their nuptials joyous and bountiful,
filling this life and the next with laughter, nighttime crickets, sounds
    of water, the descant of birdsong.

In my dream I could feel the weight of each word,
its pleasant coarseness, its heft and lug,

and so could you.
                Those who say our words are a bramble
are afraid, as children often are
when they reach into that thicket the first time
to pluck a nipple of fruit so ripe it seems drenched with the seasons
    that made it grow.
They fear thorns and wounds, and tell themselves it is impossible to
    touch the fruit, let alone taste it.

Listen to them. You need to understand
it is impossible,
                it is a miracle,
and you may savor the meaning of that word any moment you
    choose.

Reach through,
grasp what was hidden, never mind the cuts, they are part of the
    whole,
hardship joined to peace, suffering wed to joy,
and taste the promise.

The words mean just what they say.

Listen.

Acknowledgments

The author and publisher wish to thank the editors of the publications in which these poems first appeared:

32Poems: "Moonrise"
Anthology: "Wintering"
Best New Poets 2005: "One Crow, a Killing"
The Binnacle: "The Apple-Knocker"
The Christian Century: "Quandary Farm"
Encore: More of Parallel Press Poets: "Now That My Daughter Lives in the Sunlight"
Heart: "The Dream of Meanings" and "Mercy"
The Hollins Critic: "Song"
Hotmetal Press: "Dreaming in Welsh"
Listen: A Seeker's Resource for Spiritual Direction: "Tea"
The Louisville Review: "Romantic Fever" (originally titled "Fever")
Midwest Quarterly: "Lent"
Nimrod: "Specimen Collection" and "Bluesman"
North Dakota Quarterly: "October"
Plainsongs: "Forgiveness"
Poet Lore: "Summer Job"
Potomac Review: "Rappahannock"
Sonnet Writers: "River"
Southern Humanities Review: "After Donne's Devotions"
Southern Poetry Review: "Killings" (originally titled "Coming from a Meet") and "Calf-Bearer"
The Sow's Ear Poetry Review: "The Story About Horses"
The Swarthmore Literary Review: "Churches"
Tor House Newsletter: "Theory"
Virginia Quarterly Review: "Hosanna"
Water-Stone: "The Recipe"
Wisconsin Academy Review: "Considerations of Earth and Sky" and "Wharf"

"Wharf" was reprinted in *Here, Even the Blue Crabs Compose,* edited by Elisavietta Ritchie (Anthology, 2009).

"Calf-Bearer" was reprinted in *Don't Leave Hungry: Fifty Years of Southern Poetry Review,* edited by James Smith (University of Arkansas Press, 2009).

"Grace" and "The Miracle Corner" were part of a group of poems that received a 2008 Dorothy Sargent Rosenberg Prize.

"Romantic Fever" received the 2008 Samuel Dobbs Mauby Award from the Alabama State Poetry Society.

"In Passing" received the 2008 Christian Poetry Publishers Prize.

"The Dream of Meanings" received the 2008 Heart Poetry Award and was nominated for a Pushcart Prize.

"Starlings" received the 2008 "Autumn 'Boo' Award" from the Alabama State Poetry Society and was one of a group of poems that received a 2007 Dorothy Sargent Rosenberg Prize.

"Love like the Wild Geese" received the 2008 "No Name" Contest Award from the Alabama State Poetry Society.

"Hosanna" received the second place 2008 Alabama State Poetry Society Fall Contest Award.

"Moonrise" received the second place 2008 "Oil on Canvas Award" from the Alabama State Poetry Society.

"The Prodigal" received an Honorable Mention in the 2008 Utmost Christian Poetry Contest.

"The Apple-Knocker" received an Honorable Mention in the 2007 *The Binnacle* Ultra-Short Competition.

"One Crow, a Killing" was an Open Competition Winner in *Best New Poets 2005*.

"Theory" received an Honorable Mention in the 2005 Tor House Prize for Poetry.

"Considerations of Earth and Sky" received the 2003 John Lehman Award in Poetry and an Honorable Mention in the *Triplopia* Best of the Best Contest.

"Cherries" received a 1995 Academy of American Poets Award.

Thanks also to the Naval Academy Research Council for a grant which helped with portions of this book.

A number of these poems were collected in three chapbooks: *Quandary Farm* (Pudding House, 2007), *A Father's Story* (Pudding House, 2007), and *Considerations of Earth and Sky* (Parallel Press, 2005).

This full-length volume of poetry, *No Loneliness*, received the 2009 FutureCycle Poetry Book Prize.

Book design: cover by Donna Overall (donnaoverall@bellsouth.net); art by Elena Ray (elena@elenaray.com); typography by Diane Kistner (dkistner@futurecycle.org).

The FutureCycle Poetry Book Prize

FutureCycle Press is dedicated to publishing lasting English-language poetry and flash fiction books, chapbooks, and anthologies in both print-on-demand and ebook formats. Founded in 2007 by long-time independent editor/publishers and partners Diane Kistner and Robert S. King, the press incorporated as a non-profit in 2012. A number of our editors are distinguished poets and authors in their own right, and we have been actively involved in the small press movement going back to the early seventies.

The FutureCycle Poetry Book Prize and honorarium is awarded annually for the best full-length volume of poetry we publish in a calendar year. We are dedicated to giving all authors we publish the care their work deserves, making our catalog of titles the most distinguished it can be, and paying forward any earnings to fund more great books. Come see us at www.futurecycle.org.

CPSIA information can be obtained
at www.ICGtesting.com
Printed in the USA
LVOW13s0323060717

540360LV00016B/2237/P